WETLANDS

Richard Beatty

Steck-Vaughn Company

First published 2002 by Raintree Steck-Vaughn Publishers,
an imprint of Steck-Vaughn Company.
Copyright © 2002 Brown Partworks Limited

Library of Congress Cataloging-in-Publication Data

Beatty, Richard.
    Wetlands / Richard Beatty.
        p. cm. -- (Biomes atlases)
    Summary: A comprehensive look at the wetlands biome, examining its climate,
plants, animals, people, and future, plus detailed views of some famous or
important wetlands locations.
    Includes bibliographic references (p.).
    ISBN 0-7398-5251-5
    1. Wetland ecology--Juvenile literature. 2. Wetland ecology--Maps--Juvenile literature.
[1. Wetland ecology. 2. Ecology.] I. Title. II. Series.

QH541.5.M3 B43 2002
577.68--dc21

                                                        2002024841

Printed in Singapore. Bound in the United States.
1 2 3 4 5 6 7 8 9 0 LB 07 06 05 04 03 02

Brown Partworks Limited
Project Editor: Ben Morgan
Deputy Editor: Dr. Rob Houston
Consultant: Dr. L. Gordon Goldsborough,
        Director, Delta Marsh Field Station
        (University of Manitoba)
Designer: Reg Cox
Cartographers: Mark Walker and
        Darren Awuah
Picture Researcher: Clare Newman
Indexer: Kay Ollerenshaw
Managing Editor: Bridget Giles
Design Manager: Lynne Ross
Production: Matt Weyland

Raintree Steck-Vaughn
Editor: Walter Kossmann
Production Manager: Rich Johnson

Front cover: Swamp forest with aguaje palms,
Amazon Basin. *Inset*: Jacana on water lilies.

Title page: Lechwe herd, Okavango Delta,
southern Africa.

The acknowledgments on p. 64 form part of
this copyright page.

About this Book

The introductory pages of this book describe the biomes of the world and then the wetland biome. The five main chapters look at different aspects of wetlands: climate, plants, animals, people, and future. Between the chapters are detailed maps that focus on famous or important wetlands. The map pages are shown in the contents in italics, ***like this***.

Throughout the book you'll also find boxed stories or fact files about wetlands. The icons here show what the boxes are about. At the end of the book is a glossary, which explains what all the difficult words mean. After the glossary is a list of books and websites for further research and an index, allowing you to locate subjects anywhere in the book.

 Climate

 People

 Plants

 Future

 Animals

 Facts

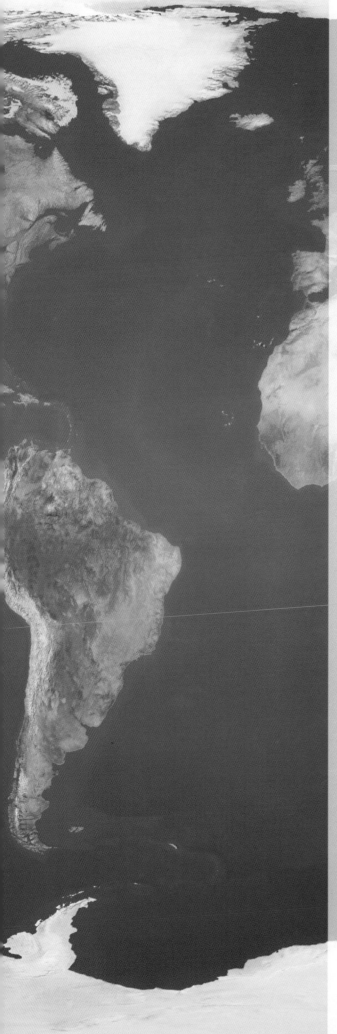

Contents

Biomes of the World

Biologists divide the living world into major zones named biomes. Each biome has its own distinctive climate, plants, and animals.

If you were to walk all the way from the north of Canada to the Amazon rain forest, you'd notice the wilderness changing dramatically along the way.

Northern Canada is a freezing and barren place without trees, where only tiny brownish-green plants can survive in the icy ground. But trudge south for long enough and you enter a magical world of conifer forests, where moose, caribou, and wolves live. After several weeks, the conifers give out, and you reach the grass-covered prairies of the central United States. The farther south you go, the drier the land gets and the hotter the sun feels, until you find yourself hiking through a cactus-filled desert. But once you reach southern Mexico, the cacti start to disappear, and strange tropical trees begin to take their place. Here, the muggy air is filled with the calls of exotic birds and the drone of tropical insects. Finally, in Colombia you cross the Andes mountain range—whose chilly peaks remind you a little of your starting point—and descend into the dense, swampy jungles of the Amazon rain forest.

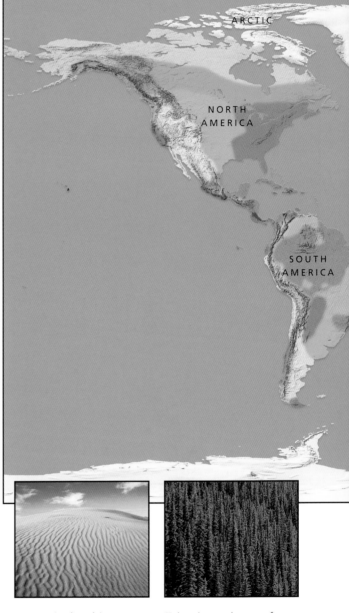

Desert is the driest biome. There are hot deserts and cold ones.

Taiga is made up of conifer trees that can survive freezing winters.

Scientists have a special name for the different regions—such as desert, tropical rain forest, and prairie—that you'd pass through on such a journey. They call them biomes. Everywhere on Earth can be classified as being in one biome or another, and the same biome often appears in lots of

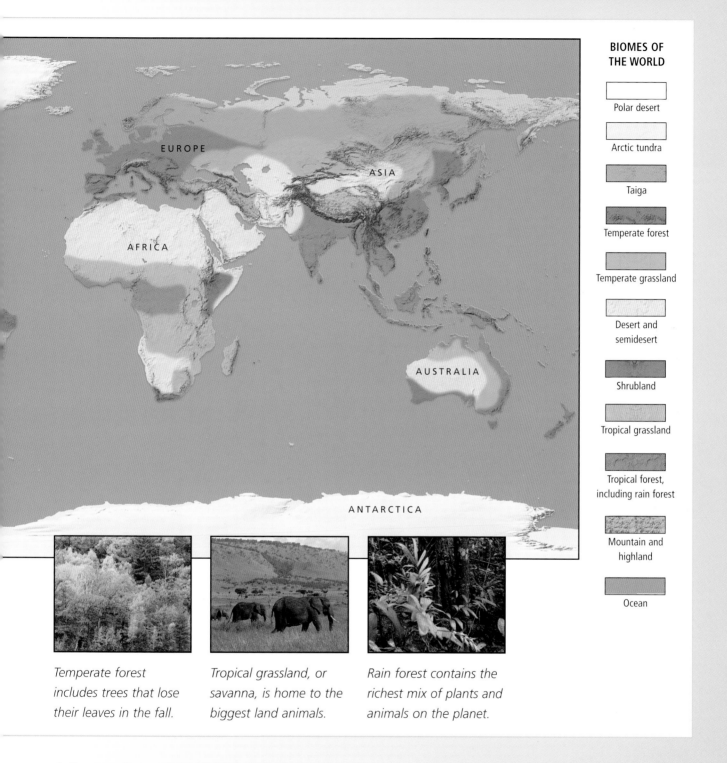

**BIOMES OF
THE WORLD**

Polar desert

Arctic tundra

Taiga

Temperate forest

Temperate grassland

Desert and
semidesert

Shrubland

Tropical grassland

Tropical forest,
including rain forest

Mountain and
highland

Ocean

EUROPE

ASIA

AFRICA

AUSTRALIA

ANTARCTICA

*Temperate forest
includes trees that lose
their leaves in the fall.*

*Tropical grassland, or
savanna, is home to the
biggest land animals.*

*Rain forest contains the
richest mix of plants and
animals on the planet.*

different places. For instance, there are areas
of rain forest as far apart as Brazil, Africa,
and Southeast Asia. Although the plants
and animals that inhabit these forests are
different, they live in similar ways. Likewise,
the prairies of North America are part of the
grassland biome, which also occurs in China,

Australia, and Argentina. Wherever there are
grasslands, there are grazing animals that feed
on the grass, as well as large carnivores that
hunt and kill the grazers.

The map on this page shows how the
world's major biomes fit together to make up
the biosphere—the zone of life on Earth.

Wetlands of the World

A wetland is a place where plants grow in soil or mud that is soaked with water. There are many different types of wetlands, from mangrove swamps to bogs and marshes.

You can find wetlands anyplace where the conditions are right, from the Arctic to the equator. Unlike deserts or rain forests, wetlands are often small areas dotted within other biomes. Some wetlands, however, are as big as a whole country.

In some wetlands, you might realize the ground is wet only if you try to run across it. In others, the whole area may be submerged under shallow water. A shallow-water wetland full of trees is called a swamp, while one with only small plants, like reeds, is called a marsh. In cold, rainy places, a type of wetland called a bog can form, making the ground wet and spongy. Rivers and lakes are not wetlands, although many have wetlands around their edges.

Wetlands also occur next to the sea. Trees called mangroves form swamp forests on tropical shores, while in cooler regions, smaller wetland plants form salt marshes.

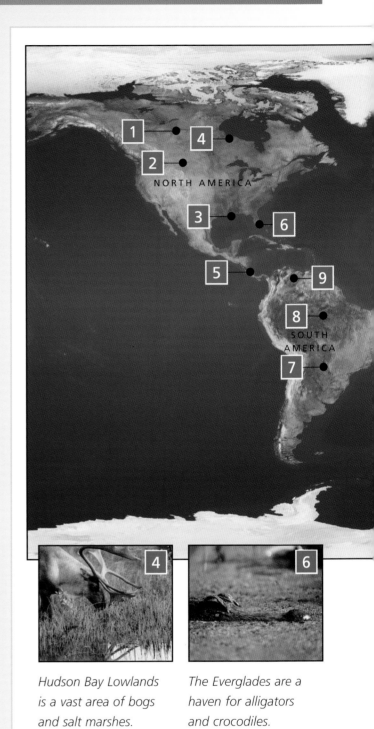

NORTH AMERICA

SOUTH AMERICA

Hudson Bay Lowlands is a vast area of bogs and salt marshes.

The Everglades are a haven for alligators and crocodiles.

Wetlands are very important for wildlife. In terms of the number of species of animals and plants, the wetland biome is second only to the tropical rain forest. For animals such as jaguars and tigers, which the growing human population has driven from drier lands, wetlands are often a safe haven.

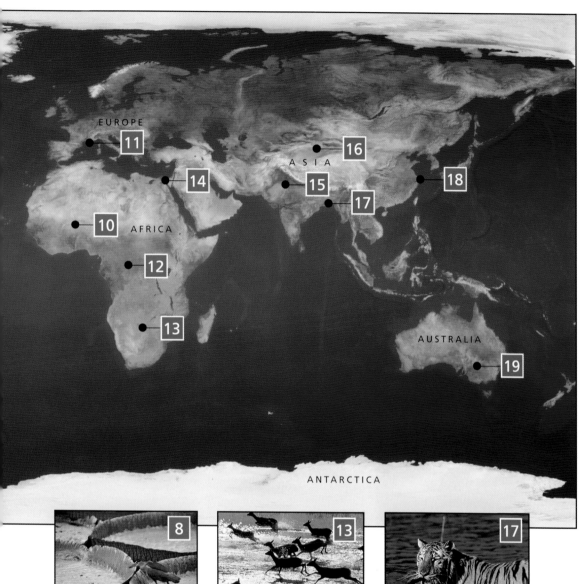

Giant water lilies grow in the many wetlands of the Amazon Basin.

The Okavango Delta is packed with wild animals, from antelope to hippos.

Mangrove swamps and tigers flourish in Asia's magnificent Sundarbans.

For centuries, people thought of wetlands as unhealthy, mosquito-filled swamps, of no use to anyone. Many wetlands were destroyed or changed in some way. Some were drained and turned into dry farmland, while others were reshaped for growing rice—a wetland plant that feeds half the world's population.

Today, people are beginning to think differently about wetlands. Besides protecting wildlife, wetlands can purify our water, help stop floods, and protect coastlines against erosion. The United States and many other countries are now making a great effort to preserve and restore their wetlands.

Hudson Bay Lowlands

The marshy plains to the south and west of Hudson Bay form one of the world's largest wetland areas. Frozen for most of the year, it thaws and springs to life in summer.

Caribou have little problem wading through the soggy ground, thanks to their splayed hooves, which are equally useful on snow. Also called reindeer, caribou are the only deer in which both sexes have antlers.

Fact File

▲ More than 99 percent of the Hudson Bay Lowlands is unspoiled wilderness.

▲ 50–75 percent of the Hudson Bay Lowlands is wetland. The rest is covered in small plants typical of the tundra biome.

▲ The wetlands include peat bogs, shallow pools, river floodplains, and coastal salt marshes.

▲ The Lowlands are part of the traditional homeland of the Cree people, who have special rights to hunt and trap wild animals.

1. Hudson Bay
The rich marine wildlife in this icy sea includes whales, seals, and walruses. It is named for the English explorer Henry Hudson, who disappeared here in 1611 after his crew mutinied and cast him adrift in a boat.

2. Churchill
Canada's northernmost seaport has no road links but can be reached by air, rail, or sea. The population is about 1,000.

3. Salt marshes
Vast salt marshes fringe the southern coast of the bay.

4. Polar Bear Provincial Park
A protected area, home to the most southerly polar bears in the world and migrating birds.

5. James Bay Hydropower Schemes
Massive dams constructed on rivers near James Bay have disrupted the environment of the Cree people and led to buildup of mercury pollution in the food chain.

6. Saskatchewan River
A mighty river fed by two tributaries flowing from the Rockies. It empties into Lake Winnipeg via Grand Rapids.

7. James Bay
This bay has two important bird sanctuaries at its southern end. Forests in the surrounding land are home to wolves, black bears, and moose.

8. Lake Winnipeg
Glaciers carved out this lake during the Ice Age. The word winnipeg means "murky waters" in the Cree language.

9. Wabakimi Provincial Park
A mixture of forest and bare rock, home to the rare woodland caribou.

GREENLAND

NORTH AMERICA

NUNAVUT

Southampton
Island

N

Coats Island →

Mansel Island

Ungava
Peninsula

● Whale Cove

● Arviat

1

Hudson Bay

Inukjuak ●

SASKATCHEWAN

2 ● Churchill

Churchill River

Nelson River

3

salt marshes

Hudson Bay Lowlands

● Fort Severn

Thompson ●

Cedar Lake

MANITOBA

4 Polar Bear
Provincial
Park

James
Bay

7

5

Saskatchewan River

Grand
Rapids

8

Severn River

Attawapiskat River

CANADA

James Bay
Hydropower
Schemes

6

Lake
Winnipegosis

Lake
Winnipeg

Akimiski
Island

ONTARIO

QUEBEC

*This satellite
picture shows
ice (white)
melting in Hudson
Bay during spring.*

9 Wabakimi
Provincial Park

Moose River

0   300 miles
0   300   km

Springing Back

Today, Hudson Bay freezes over only in winter.
Thousands of years ago, during the Ice Age—a period
when Earth's climate was much colder—both the bay
and lowlands were covered by a vast ice sheet that
pressed the land down. The ice sheet melted long ago,
but the compressed land is still rising back up at about
0.4 inches (1 cm) a year. This process creates new,
low-lying land along the coast, forming salt marshes.

UNITED
STATES

9

Climate, Land, and Water

There are so many different kinds of wetlands that scientists find it hard to classify them. This great variety results from forces such as earth movements, weather, and flowing water acting together in many different ways.

Most wetlands are in low-lying areas where water collects. Low-lying land can form for a variety of reasons. Sometimes, powerful forces in Earth's crust pull the land apart, making some areas slip down. If rivers later deposit sand and mud in these sunken areas, enormous flat plains can form. The Okavango Delta in Africa formed this way.

The prairie potholes in western North America formed in a different way. These are thousands of small, roughly circular wetland areas near the United States–Canada border. But what are they doing there? It turns out that, at the end of the Ice Age, huge blocks of ice were left stranded, sunken into the land. Eventually they melted, and the holes that remained became the prairie potholes.

Weather and Climate

The water in most wetlands comes from rain. Many bogs develop only where there is plenty of rain throughout the year. At the other extreme, some desert wetlands spring briefly to life only when there is a sudden rainstorm, which may happen just once in several years. Miraculously, plants spring from long-buried seeds, shrimps hatch from eggs, and frogs emerge from underground

Left: A herd of lechwe bound across a freshwater marsh in Africa's Okavango Delta. Okavango's marshes form where a river spreads out across a vast, flat plain.

Above: Like Okavango, the prairie potholes in North America are freshwater marshes. They formed from huge blocks of ice that melted after the Ice Age.

11

In winter the Canadian tundra is frozen solid, but in summer it melts, turning the land into a patchwork of wetlands. Canadian geese come here to breed.

chambers where they had buried themselves months before. There is a frenzy of life for a few weeks, and then the temporary wetland becomes dry and dusty once more.

By contrast, some big wetlands stay wet because rain falls on distant mountains and flows along rivers or underground to the wetland. This is why wetlands sometimes develop in the middle of deserts. Many wetlands grow and shrink with the seasons, especially in tropical countries that have a rainy and a dry season. In the rainy season, a large wetland can grow to thousands of square miles, only to shrink when the water supply dwindles. To survive, animals and plants have to be able to cope with these massive changes year after year.

The weather has many other effects on wetlands. Ice and snow, for example, are a major factor in cooler countries. Snow melting in spring can lead to the sudden

flooding of wetland areas around rivers, and if an ice jam forms, the water can spread even wider. Ice along the edges of lakes and rivers can tear their banks away, so only small, quick-growing plants can survive there. In tundra regions, such as northern Alaska and northern Canada, ice is present all year as a layer of permanently frozen ground, or permafrost, a few inches below the surface. Water can't drain away, so the whole tundra becomes a kind of boggy wetland, dotted with pools of water.

Tropical wetlands rarely see snow or ice, but other, more catastrophic weather conditions can affect them. During a dry season, lightning can trigger wildfires, even in wetlands. In the Florida Everglades, wildfires have a major influence on the plant life by encouraging the growth of small plants instead of trees. Hurricanes, too, regularly hit wetlands throughout the tropics. Their violent winds flatten tall trees and create a patchwork of different habitats in which more varied plants can flourish.

Wet and Smelly

If you go to a marsh or swamp, such as this cypress swamp in Louisiana, one of the first things you'll notice is that the soil is wet, smelly, and often under several feet of water. This is what makes a wetland a wetland. In dry soils there are spaces between the soil particles where air can circulate—including the vital gas oxygen, which plant roots and animals in the soil need to breathe. In wetlands, however, all these soil spaces are filled with water. Although oxygen molecules (the tiny particles of the gas) can dissolve in water, they move through it much more slowly than in air. Also, bacteria in the wet soil may use up what little oxygen there is. All wetland plants have to be able to cope with soil containing little or no oxygen—otherwise they will die.

Rivers and Floods

Many of the world's biggest wetlands occur around large rivers, especially where these flow through flat plains. Such rivers—the Mississippi, for example—tend to flow in a winding, or meandering, course. With time, the river shifts its position, leaving marshes and oxbow lakes where it used to flow. If the river carries a lot of sediment (mud), this settles in the wetlands. River sediment is rich in nutrients that help plants grow.

Some wetlands, however, receive water that carries few nutrients, so only certain

The aguaje palm tree forms dense swamp forests in the Amazon Basin. Local people call it the "tree of life" because it has so many uses. They use the leaves to make roofs and hammocks, the leafstalks for rope and baskets, and the edible fruit to make flour and wine.

plants can grow there. This is the case in the Everglades, where a plant called saw grass forms vast marshes because it is able to survive with few minerals in the water. But where fertilizers leak into the Everglades from farms, other wetland plants take over, such as cattails and *Melaleuca* trees. These invaders damage the natural ecosystem.

All rivers flood from time to time, but some do it every year—on a massive scale. The most spectacular of all is the Amazon River in South America. A fifth of all the river water in the world flows down this one river, as it winds its way for several thousand

The Amazon Basin

The Amazon River and its branches flow through a gigantic area of low, flat land called the Amazon Basin. It is the largest river basin in the world, and it includes many different kinds of wetlands—as well as the tropical rain forest for which it is most famous.

The basin formed over tens of millions of years from sediment carried downstream from distant mountains. For much of this period, though, the Amazon was flowing in exactly the opposite direction

to that of today. Instead of emptying into the Atlantic, it flowed west into the Pacific Ocean. About 15 million years ago, geological forces began to build the towering mountains of the Andes, blocking the river's route to the sea. The whole basin became a huge swamp without an outlet. Eventually, the Amazon wore a hole through the older, lower mountains to the east and found its way to the Atlantic, into which it still flows today.

miles through the world's largest tropical rain forest. In the rainy season, the river bursts its banks, submerging the surrounding land under so much water that river dolphins can swim through the treetops. The trees of this amazing flooded forest are able to spend up to half of each year underwater, and a unique range of animals live among them, including caimans, manatees, piranhas, and giant anacondas—the world's largest snakes.

Bogs

Not all wetlands are flat, marshy places covered in water. Bogs are special types of wetlands that form in cool parts of the world, such as Canada and northern Europe. You don't just find them on flat land but also on the sloping sides of hills and mountains. Bogs get most of their water directly from rain, rather than from rivers or through the ground. Rain contains very few nutrients, so the water in bogs tends to be infertile. It also tends to be acidic. Only certain plants, especially mosses, can cope with these conditions. One moss, sphagnum, is so good at soaking up water like a sponge that some bogs become raised up above the level of the surrounding gound.

A fen is similar to a bog, but its water comes from the ground rather than just from rain. As a result, fens tend to be more fertile than bogs, with more varied plant life.

 # Ghostly Gases

Most organisms get their energy by combining food molecules inside their bodies with oxygen from the air—a process called respiration. Just as wood releases energy when it burns in air, so food in your body releases energy when it combines with oxygen. In wetland soils, though, there is almost no oxygen, so microorganisms called bacteria use a different chemical process to release energy from their food. It gives them less energy than if oxygen were available, but they have no choice.

Some of the waste gases produced by these bacteria have a foul odor, which is why wetlands can smell disgusting. Another waste product is the gas methane, which often bubbles up from marshes. Some people claim to have seen a ghostly light—called will-o-the-wisp or jack-o'-lantern—flickering over marshes in the dead of night. It might be the methane catching fire.

River Deltas

Where a river meets the sea, the water slows down and drops its sediment, which forms a delta—an area of flat land that grows out from the shore. Not all rivers form deltas; it depends on factors such as tides and ocean currents. Deltas often contain a rich mixture of freshwater and saltwater wetlands. Some deltas are useful for farming, and many have been drained. If less sediment comes down the river because of dams, a delta may shrink. This has happened to the Nile Delta in Egypt and the Mississippi Delta in Louisiana (right).

In bogs and fens, dead plant matter tends not to decay and simply stays put. There are various reasons why decay doesn't happen. One is that the waterlogged ground stops air from getting in, which means there is not enough oxygen for microorganisms to break down the dead plants completely. Over the years, dead plant matter builds up into a dense, black substance called peat. Peat can also form in tropical swamps, where it consists mainly of undecayed tree parts.

Some bogs contain peat that is thousands of years old. The remains of ancient plants in the lower layers have enabled scientists to study what Earth's environment was like in the distant past. Dead prehistoric people have even been found in peat bogs—some so well preserved that scientists could tell what their last meals were.

Tollund Man's body lay in a Danish peat bog for 2,000 years. He was so well preserved that his stubble is still visible—as is the leather noose that was used to strangle him.

Salt marshes fringe the English coast near the village of Bosham in Sussex. One of the most common plants here is cordgrass (also called Spartina*).*

In countries such as Ireland, people have long used peat as a fuel, like firewood. More recently, however, removal of peat has developed on an industrial scale, causing much concern about ecological damage. For hundreds of years, people have also made use of a kind of fossil peat. Millions of years ago, this peat became buried deep underground, where heat and pressure slowly converted it into a hard, rocklike fuel: coal.

On the Coast

Coastal wetlands, such as salt marshes and mangrove swamps, form on low-lying coasts where rivers or sea currents deposit fine sediments in which plants can grow. Such plants have to withstand being soaked by salty water when the tide comes in.

Salt marshes are flat areas of low-growing plants. They usually form near the upper part of a muddy shoreline, where only the highest tides reach. In cooler parts of the world especially, salt-marsh plants have to cope with both salt water from the sea and freshwater from rain and rivers. Salt marshes in hotter climates can get even saltier than the sea, because the tropical sun makes the water evaporate (turn to vapor) quickly.

Mangroves are trees that grow in dense jungles between high and low tide on tropical and near-tropical coasts, including southern Florida. They grow only in warm water and have tangles of above-ground roots that help prop them up. Mangrove swamps trap river sediment, allowing it to build up and eventually turn into dry land. But if the trees are cut down, the sea can wash the land away again. One of the world's largest mangrove swamps is the Sundarbans of the Ganges Delta of east India and Bangladesh.

Everglades

The Florida Everglades covers about 4,000 square miles (10,000 sq km) of southern Florida. The whole wetland acts like a vast, slow-moving river, formed from water flowing slowly southward over the underlying rock.

 ## Gator Holes

When the Everglades dries out during the dry season, the alligators keep comfortable by digging out their own mini-wetlands. Called gator holes, these reptile-dug ponds stay filled with water, and not only the gators benefit. Fish and salamanders take refuge there, birds hunt the fish, and mammals come for a drink—though they all risk ending up in the gator's stomach. When the rainy season arrives, the rest of the marsh fills with water again and the animals scatter.

Ten Thousand Islands (above), where the land breaks up into mangrove-covered islands, is a beautiful, unspoiled wilderness, home to manatees, ospreys, and marine turtles.

 ## Fact File

▲ The word *everglade* means a grassland covered with slow-moving water. The Florida Everglades is famous for such grass-filled rivers.

▲ Saw grass, a sedge with razor-sharp leaves that can grow taller than a person, is the main type of grass in the Everglades.

▲ In the dry season, from November to May, the marshes dry out and wildfires are common.

▲ Thunderstorms are the source of most of the freshwater in the Everglades.

FLORIDA

Lake Okeechobee

Caloosahatchee River

Borrow Canal

West Palm Beach Canal

West Palm Beach

Hillsboro Canal

Miami Canal

North New River Canal

[1] Farmland

Immokalee Seminole reservation

Big Cypress Seminole reservation

Filtration marshes

[2]

Alligator Alley

Fort Lauderdale

[3]

Big Cypress National Preserve

Filtration marshes

Naples

Tamiami Canal

Tamiami Trail

Turner River Canoe Trail

Road from Miami

Miami

Ten Thousand Islands

Mangrove swamps

[6]

[5]

Saw grass marshes

[4]

Shark River Slough

Saw grass marshes

[7]

Pinelands

Visitor centre

Everglades National Park

[8]

Key Largo

Pennekamp State Park

[9]

Key
— Park boundary
— Road
— Canal
— Canoe trail

Cape Sable

Florida Bay

[10]

NORTH AMERICA

Park boundary

Florida Keys

N

0   50 miles
0   50   km

1. Farmland
The small dark squares to the south of Lake Okeechobee are agricultural fields.

2. Filtration Marshes
This zone of wetlands (brown) prevents agricultural pollution from reaching the Everglades.

3. Big Cypress National Preserve
A swamp full of bald cypress trees and mangroves, home to alligators, the rare Florida puma, and many poisonous snakes.

4. Shark River Slough
A vast area of saw grass marsh covered by flowing water, forming a grassy river (brown).

5. Saw Grass Marshes
Large areas (gray) of the Everglades are dominated by saw grass, a plant that can survive in nutrient-poor marshes.

6. Mangrove Swamps
Fringing the southwest coast of the Everglades, salt-loving mangrove trees (green) provide a sheltered habitat for many land and water animals.

7. Pinelands
Forests containing slash pine trees (bright green) grow on patches of high ground. This unique ecosystem depends on natural fires, which kill plants that would otherwise take over.

8. Everglades National Park
The area within the boundary was designated a national park in 1947, and became a World Heritage Site in 1989.

9. Pennekamp State Park
The United States' first marine park, famous for its coral reef and seagrass meadows.

10. Florida Bay
An important nursery area for the young of fish, lobsters, and other sea creatures. The bay is also home to dolphins, turtles, and manatees.

Wetland Plants

Plants have many ways of surviving in wetlands. Some prop themselves up in the soft ground with huge, stabilizing roots, while others simply float on water. To make sure they get enough nutrients, some wetland plants are meat eaters.

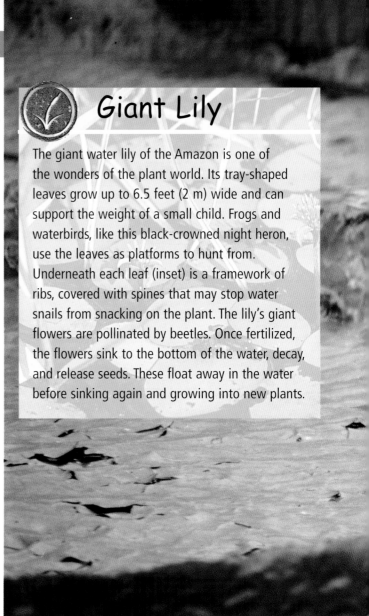

Giant Lily

The giant water lily of the Amazon is one of the wonders of the plant world. Its tray-shaped leaves grow up to 6.5 feet (2 m) wide and can support the weight of a small child. Frogs and waterbirds, like this black-crowned night heron, use the leaves as platforms to hunt from. Underneath each leaf (inset) is a framework of ribs, covered with spines that may stop water snails from snacking on the plant. The lily's giant flowers are pollinated by beetles. Once fertilized, the flowers sink to the bottom of the water, decay, and release seeds. These float away in the water before sinking again and growing into new plants.

Plants give a wetland its unique character. Think of a reedy lake shore in winter—the dead yellow stalks standing 10 feet (3 m) high, hissing as the cold wind passes through them. Or imagine rowing up a creek in a mangrove swamp, surrounded by a tangle of half-submerged mangrove roots. In the hot, still air, the only sound you'd hear would be an occasional plop—a mangrove seedling falling off its parent tree and spearing itself, root-first, in the mud below.

Many millions of years ago, horsetails (left) grew as tall as trees and formed dense forests. Today they are much smaller and only grow in wetlands, river banks, or other damp places.

Life in the Water

Scientists think most wetland plants evolved from plants that lived on dry land, but they have been in water a very long time. Water lilies, for example, probably evolved from land plants around 100 million years ago—so they have had plenty of time to get used to life in the water.

Plants cope with the challenge of living in a soggy or flooded habitat in a variety of ways. In bogs, which are cold and contain few nutrients, plants tend to be small and low-growing, such as sphagnum moss. In shallow parts of marshes, many plants have roots and stems underwater but leaves in the air. Biologists call these plants emergents.

Many reeds and sedges are emergents, as are irises and strange-looking plants called horsetails. Horsetails have stiff, jointed stems and such tiny leaves that they look leafless. They have existed since before the age of dinosaurs and once grew as big as trees, but modern horsetails are much smaller. Their stems are rough and gritty like sandpaper, and were once used for scouring dirty dishes.

Plants with floating leaves, such as water lilies, flourish in relatively still, permanent water. Such plants are kept afloat by air spaces inside their leaves and stems. The roots of water lilies are anchored in mud on the bottom, but other floating plants let their roots dangle in the water. Deeper down, some plants live entirely submerged, such as water milfoils and hornworts. Such plants usually collapse in a heap when you fish them out—they have no need for strong stalks because the water itself supports them.

Some trees can put up with being waterlogged, at least for part of the time. To prop themselves up in the soft mud, many have sturdy, above-ground roots that spread out from the trunk. The bald cypresses that grow in the swamps of the southern United States support themselves like this, as do mangrove trees and palm trees called screwpines. Screwpines don't grow wild in the United States, but one type—the candelabrum tree—is a common sight in gardens, especially in the south.

Sea of Reeds

Visit a marshland anywhere in the world and you're likely to find large areas covered with tall, grassy plants that wave in the breeze. Many are members of the grass

Living Islands

In some wetlands, floodwaters can raise living plants to form enormous floating meadows. In Africa, a special kind of floating meadow forms from papyrus plants, whose underwater stems detach from the bottom and float just below the water surface. These papyrus islands drift across open waters and lakes and sometimes clog up harbors. In wetlands of the Amazon, floating meadows can hold together for months, providing shelter for the frogs, fish, and other animals that live on or beneath them. When the floodwaters drop, the islands sink and the plants decay.

family, such as the common reed. This giant grass can grow 10 feet (3 m) high—almost twice as tall as a person—and has long, feathery flower heads. It is one of the most widespread plants in the world, common in wetlands from the Arctic to the tropics.

A related family, the sedges, includes the saw grass of the Florida Everglades, the famous papyrus plant of Africa, and many smaller species. A third family consists of plants that, from a distance, look like cigars on the ends of sticks. They also have distinctive, ribbonlike leaves around the stick. These plants, the cattails, dominate many marshes in North America. What all these plants have in common is a growth pattern that serves them well in their wetland habitats. It is based on the development of thick underground stems that can spread sideways though mud at the bottom of a marsh. These stems

The spectacular swamp hibiscus (swamp rosemallow) is native to wetlands of the southeast United States. Its huge pink flowers measure 10 inches (25 cm) wide.

last from year to year, but every year they send up fresh side shoots, which are the parts we see above the water level. The shoots collect the sun's energy and use it to make food, which passes down to the underground stem. In winter or the dry season, the shoots die, but the food they made is stored underground, ready for next year's growth. Deep beneath the mud, the stems are safe from fire, ice, or hungry animals. By growing

The spreading base of this cypress tree in Okefenokee Swamp, Georgia, helps stabilize it in the soft ground.

sideways, the stems can colonize new areas, ready to produce new shoots quickly before other plants can grow.

The reeds and their relatives are pollinated by the wind, so their flowers don't need bright petals for attracting insects. Instead, their tiny flowers are packed together in

Papyrus

The papyrus plant is a large member of the sedge family, common in African marshes and waterways. It can grow up to 15 feet (4.5 m) tall, with a tassel of leaves at the top. Papyrus is famous for giving us the word paper—the ancient Egyptians flattened the stems and pressed them together to make a writing material (right). The huge pillars in some Egyptian temples were also carved to look like the papyrus plants.

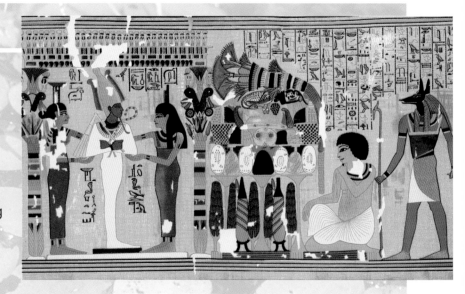

flower heads at the end of their stalks. The "cigar" of a cattail is really a mass of thousands of female flowers; the male flowers grow in a separate tassel above this. Like reeds, cattails rely on the wind to pollinate their flowers.

People have made use of plants like reeds for thousands of years, using their underground stems for food, and their leaves and shoots to make all sorts of items, from pens and musical instruments to boats and houses. The fluffy seeds of cattails have been used to stuff cushions, and you can even make a yellow cake out of their pollen.

Reeds and cattails provide shelter for many kinds of birds that nest among them. Muskrats not only build their homes from the stalks of such plants but eat them, too. But reeds can sometimes crowd out other species of plants, which is a worry to ecologists. The common reed, for example, is very important to wetland ecosystems in Europe, where

Water lilies almost cover this marsh in northern Australia's Arnhem Land, an area rich in tropical wetlands. The showy flowers attract insect pollinators.

people encourage it to grow. In the United States, however, it is spreading and choking out other wetland plants, so ecologists try to get rid of it by using chemicals, fire, or cutting it down. Since the common reed was already native to North America, it's puzzling that it is suddenly trying to take over so aggressively. Some people think it might be a different variety from abroad.

Breathing Problems

Plants need oxygen to breathe, just as we do. During the day, the green parts of plants produce their own oxygen, but their roots need to get it from the air around them. On dry land, plant roots take their oxygen from air spaces in the soil. Wetland plants, however, grow in soil that's full of water and may have no oxygen at all.

To survive, most wetland plants rely on systems of air spaces that run all the way down their stems or leafstalks and into their roots. The air spaces can also help plants stay upright or afloat. Some plants, such as water lilies, even create pressure differences in their tissues to make the air circulate faster. The air enters a young lily leaf through its stomata (tiny breathing holes), is sucked down to the underground stem, and then travels up again and out through an older leaf.

Mangrove and bald cypress trees have extra roots that can take oxygen directly from the air. Arrangements vary between species, but often the roots have knobbly branches that reach above the water surface like snorkels. Some cypress roots look just like a person's knee poking out of the water.

Sometimes it's useful to be able to do without air altogether. The underground stems of many wetland plants can manage

The Spread of Water Hyacinth

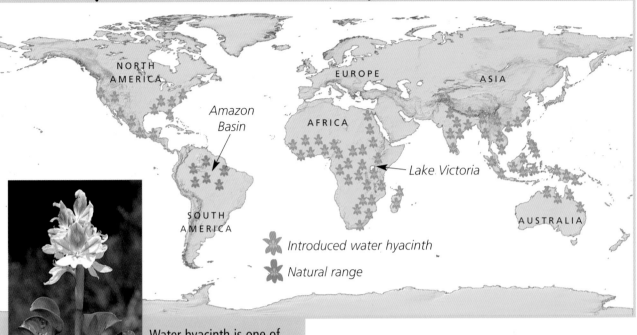

NORTH AMERICA

EUROPE

ASIA

Amazon Basin

AFRICA

SOUTH AMERICA

Lake Victoria

AUSTRALIA

✳ Introduced water hyacinth

✳ Natural range

Water hyacinth is one of the worst weeds in the world. A native of South American wetlands and lakes, it floats on the water surface, buoyed up by large air spaces in the stalk. In the 19th century, its attractive violet flowers caught the eyes of plant collectors, who took it abroad to grow in ornamental ponds and botanical gardens. It soon began spreading out of control. In Africa, it now infests nearly every river and lake, forming vast mats that choke waterways and smother the native plants. About 3 percent of the surface of Africa's vast Lake Victoria is covered by this wetland menace. It does have positive uses, though—some people harvest it by the ton to use as a fertilizer.

this during winter by altering the kinds of chemical reactions that take place inside their tissues. Instead of using oxygen to release energy from food, they carry out anaerobic (without air) reactions. These are less efficient than reactions using oxygen, but they provide just enough energy to survive until new shoots grow in the spring.

Living Together

Wetlands are often species-rich—there may be dozens of different plant species living together in a small area, competing for space. How do they all survive?

If you look carefully at the edge of a shallow lake or river, you can often see different plants growing in different places—some in soil that's only slightly damp, others in the marshy areas, and still others in deeper water. You might think that each species grows where the conditions are best for it, but the truth is more complicated than that. In fact, many wetland plants grow better in places that are much drier than where they're normally found. So why don't they grow there in the wild? The answer seems to be that other plants crowd them out, so they grow only in wetter places where the other plants can't survive.

Trees also tend to grow in particular zones in wetlands. Some trees that live near rivers can stand regular flooding, but if it floods too often, they die. In such cases, there is often a grassy wetland between the trees and river.

Many mangrove trees have upward-growing roots that take in extra air. Crabs often scuttle among them, as in this mangrove swamp in South Africa.

they reproduce, creating offspring that are all genetically unique, with different strengths and weaknesses. This variety prepares the offspring for an uncertain future, in which conditions may change. In contrast, plants arising from underground stems are genetically identical to the parent, which means they all share the same weaknesses.

In some wetlands, such as those at the edge of ponds and lakes, dead leaves and sediment may pile up year after year, gradually drying out the wetland. This allows other plants, such as trees, to start growing, and eventually the wetland may even disappear. This isn't an inevitable process, though—if there is a fire, for example, or unusually high flooding, the plants that have taken over may all be killed, and the process starts over again.

Plants often have to fight each other to survive, but they sometimes help each other. For example, some plants that are good at transporting oxygen down to their roots raise the oxygen level in the mud around them, helping other plants grow there, too.

Seeds of Change

Plants like reeds and cattails can reproduce by spreading along underground stems, so why bother to make seeds? Reproducing by seeds has several advantages for any plant. To start with, seeds are normally the product of sexual reproduction between two parents. The parents mix their genes together when

At the end of summer, cattail flowers break apart in a mass of fluff, releasing their seeds to the wind. This plant has made a useful perch for a marsh wren.

27

Some mangrove seedlings start growing while still attached to the parent plant. When they fall off, their long, spearlike roots stick into the mud.

Seeds also help a plant spread long distances. Cattails, for example, produce thousands of light, fluffy seeds that blow for miles in the wind. Birds often spread wetland plants by transporting seeds that are in the mud on their feet or have stuck to their feathers. Some grasslike plants called rushes have sticky seeds for exactly this reason. Water lilies and many other plants have seeds or fruits containing air spaces or drops of oil that allow them to float away on the water. In the flooded forests of the Amazon, floating tree fruits are an important food for fish. Sometimes the seeds inside the fruits are destroyed, but many pass through the fish unharmed, helping spread the tree's offspring through the forest.

Plunging in

Some mangrove trees produce seeds that sprout while still attached to the parent tree. The young plants may grow several feet long before they fall off. In some cases they plunge straight into the mud below, anchored by spear-shaped roots. In other cases they float away on the water and take root later on. The cannonball mangrove has a different trick. Its football-sized fruit explodes when ripe, scattering seeds in all directions.

Wetland mud often contains thousands of buried seeds, all waiting until conditions are right to start growing. Scientist call these reserves "seed banks." Some of the seeds get their chance only if a fire or hurricane destroys the plants around them, leaving a clear space for the seedling to grow in. Others can survive for years in dry ground, waiting for water to return. The seeds of the sacred lotus (a plant like a water lily) can sprout successfully after hundreds of years.

Sphagnum

Sphagnum is a specialized kind of moss that grows in bogs in cool countries. Often yellowish rather than green, it is riddled with empty spaces that give it an amazing ability to soak up rain like a sponge and keep itself wet. Like other mosses, sphagnum has no true roots but can absorb water and nutrients directly through its surface. As it slowly grows, the lower part of its stem becomes buried, dies, and turns into peat as it rots. In addition to being highly absorbent, sphagnum moss has useful disinfective properties. In the past, people collected it to use as a dressing for wounds or to make sanitary pads and diapers.

Carnivorous Plants

Plants that eat animals are called carnivorous plants. Like carnivorous animals, they eat flesh—but not to obtain energy. A clue to why carnivorous plants evolved comes from the fact that most of them live in boggy areas where the waterlogged soil contains very few nutrients. But insects contain nutrients—especially the vital nitrates that the plants need to make proteins. By trapping insects, carnivorous plants can supplement their nitrate intake and survive where other plants would perish.

Carnivorous plants use a range of traps to capture and kill their prey. Pitcher plants have cup-shaped leaves that partly fill with rain. If an insect falls in, slippery walls and backward-pointing hairs stop it from escaping. The victim soon drowns, and the plant digests it. Pitchers are widespread in North American wetlands, but the largest ones live in Southeast Asia. These are said to trap lizards and frogs as well as insects.

Below: Lacewings are easy prey for sundew plants because their large wings quickly get stuck. If the lacewing struggles, more blobs of glue will stick to it.

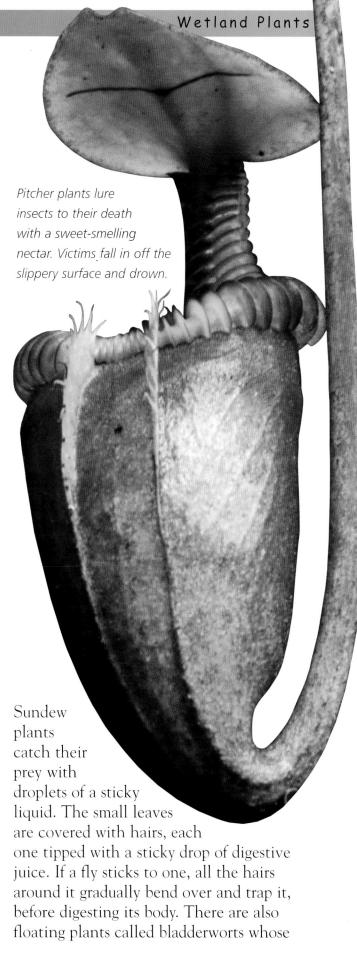

Pitcher plants lure insects to their death with a sweet-smelling nectar. Victims fall in off the slippery surface and drown.

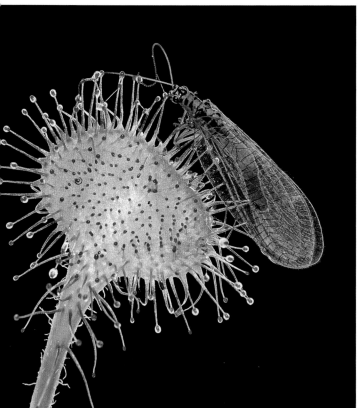

Sundew plants catch their prey with droplets of a sticky liquid. The small leaves are covered with hairs, each one tipped with a sticky drop of digestive juice. If a fly sticks to one, all the hairs around it gradually bend over and trap it, before digesting its body. There are also floating plants called bladderworts whose

underwater leaves grow tiny, cup-shaped chambers, or bladders. If a water flea or other tiny aquatic animal bumps into a bladder, a trapdoor swings open, the victim gets sucked inside, and the door snaps shut over it.

Probably the most remarkable carnivorous plant is the Venus's-flytrap, a native of the Carolinas. People often grow this vicious insect-killer as a houseplant. Its leaves are hinged across the middle to form a pair of

Mangrove swamps (below, red) grow on tropical coastlines, especially in sheltered waters.

rounded lobes, each fringed with spiny teeth. When an insect lands on one of the lobes, they shut together and the teeth interlock to form a deadly cage. A clever trigger mechanism stops the trap from shutting accidentally—there are three trigger hairs on each lobe, and an insect has to touch two in quick succession to activate the trap.

Salt Water

The plants of salt marshes have a lot to contend with. Besides getting completely flooded from time to time by the tides, they have to cope with a water supply that is sometimes salty and sometimes fresh. Not many plants can survive in these conditions, but one that can is cordgrass, a grass whose seeds will sprout only in salty water. Another is an odd plant named glasswort or samphire, which has juicy, succulent stems that are

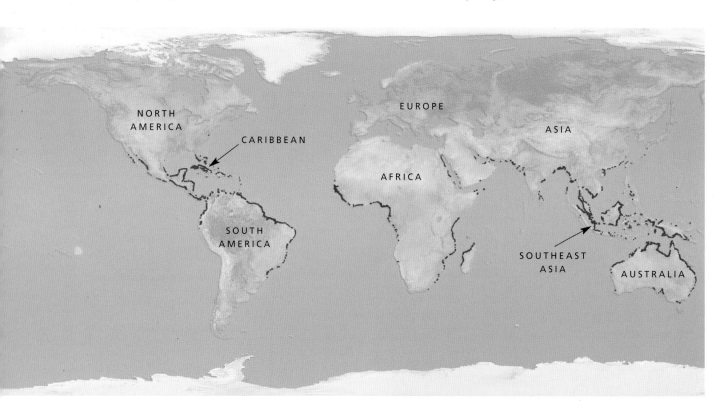

NORTH AMERICA

CARIBBEAN

SOUTH AMERICA

EUROPE

ASIA

AFRICA

SOUTHEAST ASIA

AUSTRALIA

edible. It is named glasswort because people used to burn the plant and then use the ashes in glass making.

In warmer parts of the world, you often find mangrove swamps growing in place of salt marshes. There are about sixty species of mangrove trees worldwide (depending on your definition of a mangrove). They are not all related to one another—several different plant families have evolved mangrove species. Propped up by their tangled roots, mangrove trees can form dense thickets that are extremely difficult to travel through.

Mangroves all have the problem of living in salty water. Their roots can filter salt out of seawater, but some still gets inside the plant. To get rid of it, many mangroves secrete salt through their leaves, forming a white crust. Some mangroves concentrate their salt in bark or dying leaves, which fall off the plant and take the salt with it.

Feeding the World

The rice plant is a kind of grass that grows in wetlands. People have cultivated rice for thousands of years, and half the world's people now rely on this plant as their staple food. Rice plants grow, flower, and die within a single year, so farmers have to plant a new crop every growing season. They grow it in waterlogged fields called paddies. Some farmers also release fish into the paddies and harvest these along with the rice. Mature rice plants can reach 6 feet (1.8 m) tall. The seeds—rice grains—form in large, dangling flowerheads.

The red mangrove is one of the most common American mangrove species. Its arching prop roots spread along the ground and produce new plants.

Okavango Delta

Most rivers flow into the sea, but Africa's Okavango River is different. It flows inland and ends in a vast, sun-scorched plain, where the water spreads out and evaporates. The result is the Okavango Delta—one of the wildlife wonders of Earth.

 ## Fact File

▲ Crocodiles and hippos live permanently in the delta, but many other animals visit only in the dry season to find water and fresh grazing.

▲ Lions, leopards, and cheetahs in the surrounding savannas prey on animals traveling to the delta.

▲ More than 600 bird species live in and around the Okavango Delta, from waterbirds to ostriches.

▲ The rich wildlife has made the Okavango Delta one of the world's top ecotourism destinations.

▲ Unlike other rivers that drain into deserts, the Okavango's water always remains fresh, and never becomes salty.

 ## Under Threat

The Okavango Delta is the mainstay of Botswana's tourist industry—but that doesn't mean it's safe from damage in the future. There are many pressures on the ecology of the delta, such as an increase in cattle ranching in the surrounding savannas. The ranchers have put up miles of fences to stop their cattle from catching diseases from wild animals. But these fences are a disaster for wildlife—some animals die because they can't reach the water of the delta, while others are burned to death when bush fires herd them against the fences. A few fences have been taken down again, but many still remain and cause continued disruption.

Seen from the air, the Okavango Delta is a patchwork of pools, rivers, and grassy islands. The terrain is hard to cross, which helps protect animals from predators.

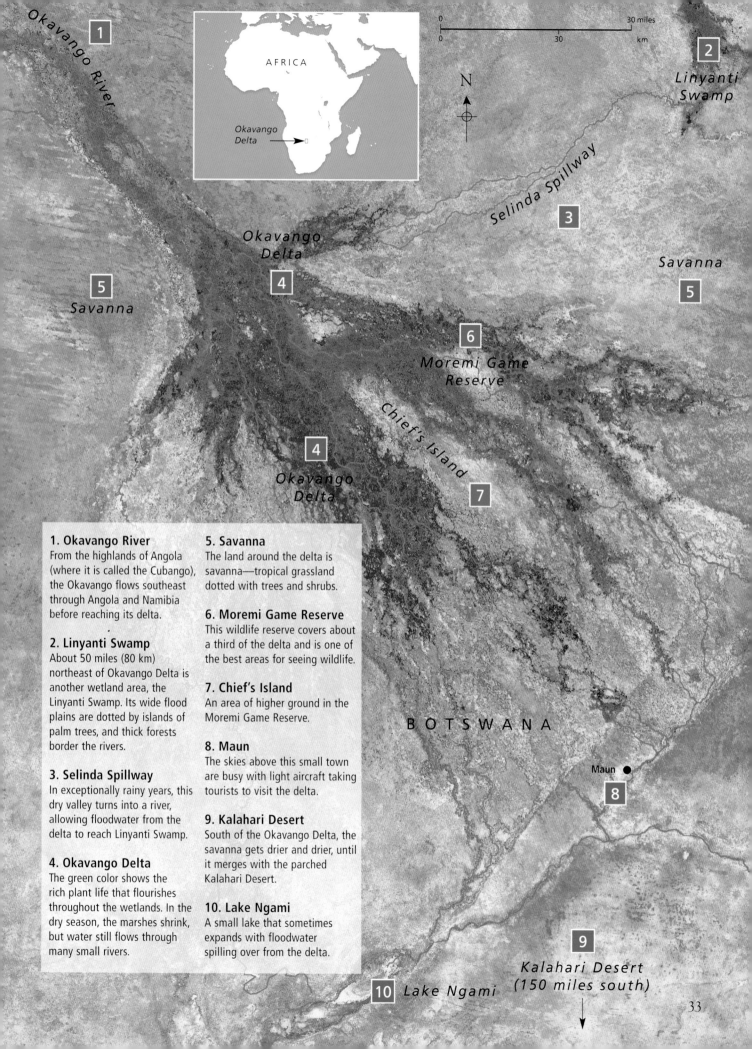

1

Okavango River

2

Linyanti Swamp

3

Selinda Spillway

5

Savanna

Okavango Delta

4

6

Moremi Game Reserve

Savanna

5

4

Okavango Delta

Chief's Island

7

B O T S W A N A

Maun ●

8

9

Kalahari Desert (150 miles south)

10 *Lake Ngami*

AFRICA

Okavango Delta

N

0   30 miles

0   30

km

1. Okavango River
From the highlands of Angola (where it is called the Cubango), the Okavango flows southeast through Angola and Namibia before reaching its delta.

2. Linyanti Swamp
About 50 miles (80 km) northeast of Okavango Delta is another wetland area, the Linyanti Swamp. Its wide flood plains are dotted by islands of palm trees, and thick forests border the rivers.

3. Selinda Spillway
In exceptionally rainy years, this dry valley turns into a river, allowing floodwater from the delta to reach Linyanti Swamp.

4. Okavango Delta
The green color shows the rich plant life that flourishes throughout the wetlands. In the dry season, the marshes shrink, but water still flows through many small rivers.

5. Savanna
The land around the delta is savanna—tropical grassland dotted with trees and shrubs.

6. Moremi Game Reserve
This wildlife reserve covers about a third of the delta and is one of the best areas for seeing wildlife.

7. Chief's Island
An area of higher ground in the Moremi Game Reserve.

8. Maun
The skies above this small town are busy with light aircraft taking tourists to visit the delta.

9. Kalahari Desert
South of the Okavango Delta, the savanna gets drier and drier, until it merges with the parched Kalahari Desert.

10. Lake Ngami
A small lake that sometimes expands with floodwater spilling over from the delta.

Wetland Animals

Wetlands are difficult for people to live in, but that makes them perfect refuges for wildlife. Some of the world's most amazing animals find sanctuary in wetlands, from man-eating crocodiles to air-breathing fish.

With eyes raised on the top of the head, crocodiles and alligators can hide in water while looking for prey. The American alligator (below) declined in number in the early 20th century, but since being protected it is now common again in the southeast United States.

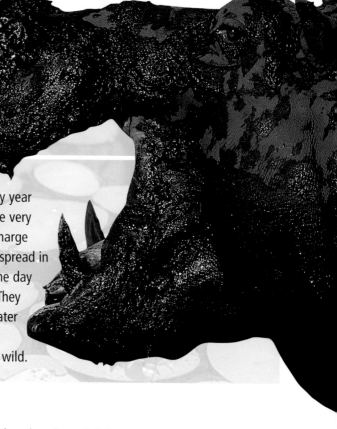

Armed and Dangerous

The most dangerous animals in Africa are not lions, hyenas, or crocodiles, but hippopotamuses. Hippos kill more people every year than any other animal. Although they are herbivores, they can be very aggressive—if you wander too close and scare a hippo, it will charge suddenly and gore you with its huge tusks. Hippos are still widespread in rivers, lakes, and wetlands in many parts of Africa. They spend the day resting in water, but at night they come onto land to eat grass. They have a complicated social life and can communicate by underwater sounds like their distant relatives, the whales. The much smaller pygmy hippo lives in tropical forests and is now very rare in the wild.

In the depths of Africa's Congo rain forest are some little-known wetland areas that are home to one of Earth's finest wildlife sights. What's so special about these marshy clearings is that the secretive animals of the forest come out into the open together—to drink, eat wetland plants, and perhaps get salts from muddy pools. Forest elephants lead their young to the water, wild pigs root around in the mud, and, strangest of all, families of gorillas emerge from the forest to eat, play, and relax in the sunshine. Sometimes there are floods, and fish such as catfish swim into the marshes from nearby streams, slithering snakelike across the drying ground as the waters fall again.

Many of the world's wetlands, just like those in central Africa, act as animal meeting points, where the lives of land and water-living animals overlap. Some species, like hippos and crocodiles, are permanent residents, but others are visitors. In Africa, herds of antelope trek hundreds of miles to wetlands in the dry season to find fresh grass. An animal may visit a wetland for many reasons—perhaps just to cool off, or to hide

Manatees are large, plant-eating animals that live in sluggish rivers, mangrove swamps, and coastal shallows. Defenseless against both hunters and boat propellers, they are now endangered.

Because wetlands attract animals from far and wide, they harbor some of the richest wildlife on Earth. Add to this the fact that wetlands are often more unspoiled than the dry lands around them, and it's easy to see why wetlands are some of the most important areas for wildlife conservation on the planet. For the wetland animals themselves, though, life is always a challenge—they must find food and shelter, avoid being eaten, and produce the next generation successfully.

Capybaras, the world's biggest rodents, live in herds in South American wetlands. The babies purr to stay in touch with their mothers.

Looking for a Meal

Animals rely ultimately on plants for food. They may be plant eaters themselves or they may eat the animals that eat the plants, and so on. Often it's the dead plants that are most important to the wetland food chain. Leaves and stalks fall into the water and begin to decay, providing food for aquatic insects and small, shrimplike animals. In turn, these are eaten by fish, frogs, and birds.

Some wetland animals do eat live plants, though. These include grazers like the moose, which often wades in the marshes of its northern homeland for food. A more specialized animal is the capybara of South America, a sort of giant guinea pig with

partly webbed feet. Its eyes and nose are on the top of its head, so it can see and breathe as it swims. Capybaras live in small herds and eat many wetland plants, including those that form floating meadows during the wet season. The floating meadows are also food for the Amazonian manatee, a massive, slow-moving mammal that lives entirely in water. Manatees look a bit like small whales, but they're more closely related to elephants. Some fish, too, rely mainly on plant food, such as fruits that fall from nearby trees.

Many wetland animals, such as turtles, are omnivores—they eat both animal and plant food. Others are specialized predators. At the top of the food chain are the biggest wetland predators of all: crocodiles and alligators. Crocodiles hunt by stealth, hiding in the water and waiting until a suitable victim comes close. When a small animal such as a monkey comes close to the water's edge for a

It might sound impossible, but anacondas can swallow caimans whole. The bones in the snake's jaw dislocate, allowing the mouth to stretch around massive prey.

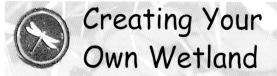

Creating Your Own Wetland

When a beaver builds its dam, it creates a wetland for other species, as well as for itself. The lakes that form behind beaver dams kill the trees growing there, and wetland plants soon colonize the lake edges. Even if the dam collapses or the beavers abandon it, the flooded area is likely to stay marshy for years, until the trees finally take over again. Before Europeans arrived in North America and started hunting beavers, there were up to 400 million of them on the continent—that made for a lot of wetland!

Horrible Diseases

Wetlands are fascinating places, but they have a dark side. If you're unlucky, especially in the tropics, you might catch a horrible disease there. Malaria and yellow fever are spread by bloodsucking mosquitoes (right), whose larvae live in still, swampy waters. Schistosomiasis is a disease caused by parasitic worms that live in wetlands. The young worms begin life inside the bodies of snails, but then leave their hosts and become free-swimming. If you paddle in water containing these worms, they will burrow through your skin and set up home inside your body, causing an itchy rash ("swimmer's itch") or more serious symptoms.

drink, the crocodile sweeps it off its feet with a lash of the tail and snatches it in its mouth. Another top predator is the anaconda of South America—the world's heaviest snake. It hides in wetlands, slipping silently through the water in search of capybaras and caimans. It kills by constriction, coiling around the victim and crushing its lungs to suffocate it. Then the snake swallows the body whole.

The Art of Wetland Living

Wetlands may not sound as difficult to live in as deserts or icy tundra, but they have their own challenges. For land animals, one obvious problem is how to walk around

Bloodsuckers

If you ever take a walk through a tropical wetland, you'll probably find something nasty stuck to your ankles when you get your boots off: leeches. These bloodsucking worms can slip under clothes and into shoes. They fasten themselves to your skin with suckerlike mouths and secrete a painkiller so you hardly notice them. Some leeches suck only the blood of fish or frogs, but others prefer larger animals, including people. Certain types of leeches are used in medicine, especially to get rid of blood that has collected in swellings. The world's biggest leech, which lives in the Amazon, grows to about 18 inches (46 cm) long.

Sticky feet allow African reed frogs to walk straight up vertical surfaces. Reed frogs have brightly patterned skin and some can change color from hour to hour.

without getting feet stuck in the mud. Several kinds of deer have feet that spread out when they put their weight on them; a marsh-living rabbit uses the same trick. Other animals, including ducks and otters, have webbed feet that they can use for both walking and swimming. Some insects are famous for their ability to walk on water, using the force of the water's surface (or surface tension) to hold them up. Birds called jacanas have amazingly long toes that spread their weight widely, allowing them to walk on water lilies without sinking.

One group of animals that specialize in living on both land and water are the amphibians, the group that includes frogs and salamanders. Wetlands are major habitats for

amphibians. Their young (such as tadpoles) usually live in water and breathe through gills, while adults generally live on land. The adults prefer damp habitats because they need to keep their skin moist. The wetlands of North America support a rich diversity of amphibians—according to one estimate, Tennessee has more salamander species than the whole of Europe and Asia.

One of the biggest challenges of wetland life is coping with seasonal changes. Some wetlands are flooded for half the year but dry up for the other half. Birds and many insects can simply fly away when things get difficult, but other animals have to be more careful. In the rainy season, both the Amazon and Congo rivers flood the surrounding forests,

Jacanas can use their long legs as stilts to wade through shallow water. They also have long toes and wide feet for walking on water lilies.

allowing fish to swim through the trees in search of food. When the water level drops, the fish must be sure to return to the river. Ground-living insects of the forest floor face the opposite problem, so they migrate into the treetops when the forests begin to flood.

The lungfish of Africa, Australia, and South America stay put when their wetland habitat dries out. Before the water disappears, they dig themselves into the mud and cocoon their bodies in a protective membrane, sealed so only the lips are showing. They stay like this for months, immobile but alive and breathing air, until the rains return and their pools fill up again. Lungfish are an ancient group and may be closely related to the first amphibians. People have found fossils of lungfish that died in their burrows more than 100 million years ago.

Scarlet ibises live in the wetlands and coastal mudflats of South America and the Caribbean. Their vivid color comes from the shrimps they eat.

Long, curved bill for probing water and mud.

Stiltlike legs for wading.

Long, spreading toes for walking on mud.

Waterbirds

One of the main reasons people try to conserve wetlands is to safeguard the many birds that live there. Wetlands have some of the densest populations of birds on the planet. Most of these birds migrate, and if a particular wetland is drained or destroyed, this can seriously disrupt their patterns of migration.

A huge variety of bird species make use of wetlands. Probably the most spectacular are the large wading birds, such as herons, storks, cranes, and ibises. The scarlet ibis of the Caribbean and South America must count as one of the most eye-catching birds in the world. Wetlands are also home to more familiar swimming birds, such as ducks, geese, and grebes. Other wetland specialists are the rails—shy, sometimes nocturnal (night-active) birds that hide among the reeds. Kingfishers, which dive to catch fish, earn a good living in wetlands, as do hawks, eagles, and other birds of prey.

Above: Herons use their sharp eyes to spot fish and a daggerlike bill to skewer them. They curve the long neck back in an S-shape before making a strike.

You can often get a clue about what wetland birds eat from the kind of bills they have. For example, long, thin bills are usually used for picking out small creatures from mud or under stones. Herons have daggerlike bills for stabbing fish, while the aptly named spoonbill sifts food from muddy water with sweeping movements of its bill. Geese have strong, stout bills for tearing the plant food that they mainly live on. Many ducks have a kind of sieve inside their beaks to strain food from the water, while other duck species have narrow beaks with sawtooth edges for catching fish.

Perhaps the most unusual beak of a wetland bird is that of the shoebill, or whale-headed stork, of Africa. This bird uses its gigantic bill to dig lungfish out of their burrows and snatch fish from the water.

Wetlands are great places for bird-watchers because vast numbers of birds often gather in a small area. At breeding time, the birds may put on a spectacular show as males and females

Shoebills live in papyrus swamps in east Africa. Despite their fierce appearance, they are quiet, patient birds that stand almost motionless for hours, waiting to ambush fish and other prey.

41

A Tale of Two Dolphins

Not all dolphins live in the sea. Several species live in freshwater, including two that live in the Amazon River. These two species are very different from one another, though. One is closely related to marine dolphins, while the other belongs to a unique group called the river dolphins. The Amazon river dolphin (right) is almost blind, with a long, thin nose and a neck that can bend. Its flexible shape allows it to leave the river and hunt fish among the tangle of underwater branches when the forest is flooded. In contrast, the other Amazon dolphin is not equipped to maneuver among branches, so it has to stay behind in the main river.

Left: Archerfish use a well-aimed squirt of water to dislodge prey. They live in mangrove swamps, where insects are common in overhanging plants.

court each other. Cranes are especially famous for their courtship dances, which may include leaping off the ground, hopping on one leg, flapping the wings, and making loud trumpeting noises. For breeding birds, wetlands have the advantage that nests built among reeds or on small islands are relatively safe from predators. Many species, especially geese, breed in wetlands of the tundra in northern Canada and Europe. The long summer days and plentiful insect food in the tundra help their chicks grow fast.

Scientists have tracked the movements of wetland birds by tagging them with harmless metal leg-rings. These studies have revealed that there are major "flyways" followed by millions of migrating birds. The main flyways in North America are the east coast, the west coast, and the Mississippi valley. If wetlands along these routes were destroyed, birds would not be able to stop and refuel on their long journeys, and might die out as a result.

Animals of Swamps and Mangroves

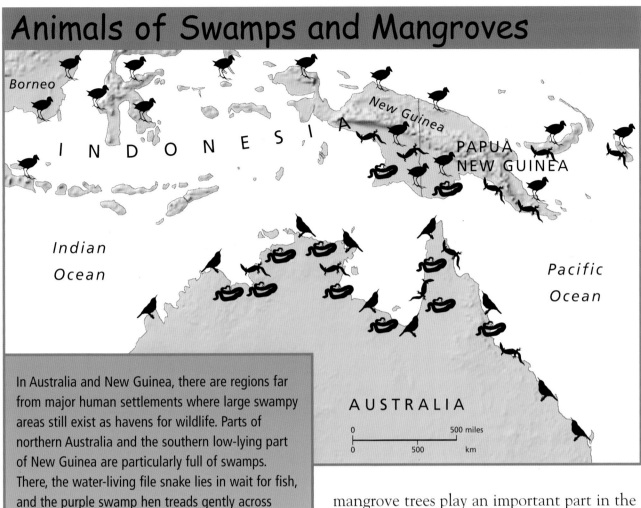

Borneo

New Guinea

INDONESIA

PAPUA NEW GUINEA

Indian Ocean

Pacific Ocean

AUSTRALIA

0   500 miles

0   500   km

In Australia and New Guinea, there are regions far from major human settlements where large swampy areas still exist as havens for wildlife. Parts of northern Australia and the southern low-lying part of New Guinea are particularly full of swamps. There, the water-living file snake lies in wait for fish, and the purple swamp hen treads gently across water lilies and lotus plants on the water surface. Different species of animals live in the salty mangrove habitats on the coasts. In Australia at least, the mangrove monitor lizard and the red-headed honeyeater rarely stray far from mangroves.

Mangrove monitor lizard

Purple swamp hen

Red-headed honeyeater

File snake

Life Among the Mangroves

Mangrove swamps are a unique habitat. They are true forests, where many land-dwelling forest creatures live. Yet they grow between high and low tide, and are invaded by the sea twice a day. The leaves that drop from mangrove trees play an important part in the swamps' ecology. They form the basis of food chains that support animals both among the mangroves and in the sea beyond.

Some mangrove animals are sea creatures that take advantage of the shelter and food to be found in the forest. In particular, two families of small crabs—the fiddler crabs and the grapsids—specialize in living in mangrove swamps throughout the world, often in huge numbers. To avoid predatory fish, crabs of both types dig burrows for themselves and stay inside while the tide is in. At low tide they emerge, the fiddler crabs to sift through mud for food, and the grapsids in search of mangrove leaves (usually dead ones), which they store and eat. Both kinds of crabs can survive out of water for a while but must return to their burrows from time to time to keep their gills moist.

The Pantanal

One of the biggest wetlands in the world is the Pantanal in South America, a marshy floodplain about as big as Oklahoma. It's not connected to the Amazon but lies farther south, near another huge river called the Paraguay. Cattle graze on the Pantanal in the dry season, but when the rains

come, the land floods with shallow water. Patches of higher ground turn into small forested islands, dotted throughout the area.

The Pantanal provides a refuge for many of South America's most spectacular animals—not just wetland species but others, too. Among the wetland species are giant otters and huge numbers of caimans (above). These relatives of the alligator are often poached for their skins. Other animals include jaguars, giant anteaters, giant armadillos, and tapirs—large, hoofed animals with long, flexible noses. More than 700 species of birds have also been seen in the Pantanal, among them the beautiful but endangered hyacinth macaw—the biggest parrot in the world.

Male fiddler crabs are best known for having one claw that is much bigger than the other one. They wave the larger claw to send signals to other crabs—to show that they are prepared to defend their burrows from other males, for example, or to attract a mate.

Among the best-known creatures of mangrove swamps are the mudskippers—odd, frog-faced fish that can move around out of water. They do this either by flicking their tails to hop along the mud, or by levering themselves along with their front fins, in a slow walk. Mudskippers often climb up mangrove roots, perhaps to avoid larger fish below, and can

Below: mudskippers use their front fins as arms to haul themselves up stones and mangrove roots. They can also skip along mud by flicking their tail. Their bulging eyes let them see above the water surface.

breathe through their moist skin as well as through gills. There are various species, some that hunt prey actively and others that sift through mud for food.

The largest animals of mangrove swamps vary in different parts of the world. In Asia, forest animals such as deer, wild pigs, tigers, and even rhinoceroses live on the ground, while the treetops are home to monkeys and colorful birds. The extraordinary-looking proboscis monkey lives in the mangrove swamps of Borneo and specializes in eating mangrove leaves. Male proboscis monkeys are very easy to recognize—they have weird, dangly noses that reach below their chins.

In the water you might see turtles, snakes, and monitor lizards—large, flesh-eating lizards that can swim and climb well. In

Above: Proboscis monkeys' huge stomachs contain bacteria that help break down mangrove leaves. They are one of the only monkeys known to swim.

eastern Asia and Australia, there's also a far bigger and more dangerous animal: the estuarine or saltwater crocodile, the largest reptile in the world. Estuarine crocodiles normally grow to 13 feet (4 m) long, but 23-foot (7 m) males have been seen. They hunt large animals by waiting silently at the water's edge. If a buffalo, wallaby, or even a person comes too close, the crocodile lunges forward and grabs them. After drowning the victim, it spins around to tear its body apart.

Nile Delta

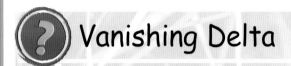

Where the mighty Nile River meets the Mediterranean Sea, it spreads out into a broad triangular plain called the Nile Delta. People have farmed the rich soils here for millennia.

? Vanishing Delta

In 1902, Egypt built a dam across the Nile River, near Aswan (above). In 1970, a bigger dam was built—the Aswan High Dam. For the first time, people could control the annual Nile floods. This has boosted the Egyptian economy, but much less river sediment now reaches the delta—and even that settles in artificial channels before reaching the sea. Sea currents and rising sea levels are also eating away at the coastal delta. Unless something is done, much of the delta may disappear.

Most of Egypt's crops are grown in the Nile Delta region. They include cotton, wheat, corn, and rice.

Fact File

▲ The Nile Delta stopped being a natural wilderness a long time ago. The ancient Egyptians, and later the Romans, used it to grow crops.

▲ Until the Aswan High Dam was completed in 1970, the Nile flooded every year. Mud deposited by the floods kept the delta's soil very fertile.

▲ Most of Egypt's human population lives in the Nile Delta or along the banks of the Nile.

▲ About a billion birds fly from Europe and India to the Nile Delta each year. Some stay for the winter, but others use it as a stop-off point on the journey farther south into Africa.

▲ The delta stretches 100 miles (158 km) south to north from Cairo to the Mediterranean; its coast is 150 miles (237 km) long and dotted with lagoons.

▲ Birds in the delta feed in marshes, lakes, and saltwater lagoons among the farmland.

Mediterranean Sea

Rosetta

1

2

Lake
Burullus

4

5

Lake
Manzala

Port Said

7

Lake
Bardawil

Nile (Damietta branch)

• Al Mansura

3

6

N

Suez Canal

Nile Delta

Nile (Rosetta branch)

Tanta •

EGYPT

Sinai
Desert

Ismailiya •

Circles
of farmland
irrigated by
Nile water.

Western
Desert

Eastern
Desert

Great
Bitter Lake

8

Cairo

AFRICA

• Suez

Al Giza •

Giza
pyramids

Red
Sea

Lake
Qarun

Al Faiyûm

9

Nile River

Aswan High Dam,
300 miles (475 km)
to the south

1. Rosetta
Near this town in 1799, a famous ancient inscribed stone was found. The Rosetta Stone enabled scholars to decipher the hieroglyphic script used by the ancient Egyptians.

2. Lake Burullus
This saltwater lagoon is a protected wetland site. It is important for wintering and migrating wetland birds.

3. Nile Delta
Half the population of the delta are small landowners called fellahin. Before the Nile was dammed, farmers could grow only one crop—sowing their seeds in the mud left after the annual flood. Now irrigation channels feed the delta year-round, allowing the fellahin to grow two or three crops.

4. Disappearing coast
Now that the Nile no longer floods, its sediment no longer reaches the sea, and the coast is eroding. The once nutrient-rich coastal waters have lost the sardine fisheries that were an important food resource.

5. Lake Manzala
The biggest saltwater lagoon in the Nile Delta once supplied a third of Egypt's fish but is now used for dumping Cairo's sewage in.

6. Suez Canal
Opened in 1869, the canal shortened the sea route between Europe and Asia by thousands of miles. The Great Bitter Lake formed when seawater flowing along the new canal flooded a low-lying area.

7. Lake Bardawil
This largely unpolluted lagoon is home to many wetland birds.

8. Cairo
The capital of Egypt has been the largest city in Africa for centuries. To the west are the pyramids at Giza, built 4,500 years ago.

9. Al Faiyûm
This low-lying area includes wetlands and Lake Qarun. It is important for wildlife and contains some early archaeological remains.

0   50 miles

0   50

km

47

People and Wetlands

Wetlands are important for people as well as for wildlife, but their benefits have not always been obvious. The more we learn about wetlands, the more we realize how important it is to protect them.

Below: In the Okavango Delta of Botswana, simple rafts made from papyrus stems provide a cheap if precarious alternative to boats.

People have made use of wetlands since the earliest times. Hunting peoples have probably always visited wetlands to take advantage of the birds, fish, and other animals that abound there. Early cattle-herders, too, most likely led their herds to wetland areas during the dry season to find fresh grass, just as they still do in parts of Africa today. Over time, some peoples

became wetland specialists and lived permanently in marshes, developing ways of life that were beautifully adapted to take advantage of what these areas have to offer.

In medieval Europe, for example, people in the fens of eastern England and the Netherlands both developed wetland cultures. They lived by farming, fishing, and hunting for waterbirds. Hunters floated wooden ducks on the water to fool real ducks into coming within catching distance—a trick the ancient Egyptians also knew about. Craftspeople used reeds for making baskets, roofing material, and many other items.

People navigated the shallow wetland waters using flat-bottomed boats that they pushed around on long poles. They

The Marsh Arabs

Since about 5,000 years ago, the wetlands of southern Iraq have been home to a people called the marsh Arabs, or *Ma'dan*. They live on islands in the marshes constructed entirely of reeds, and build elegant canoes and beautiful, arched houses out of reeds. Besides hunting and fishing, the marsh Arabs grow rice and keep herds of water buffalo tethered to their islands.

This unique way of life is disappearing quickly. Like the Kurds in northern Iraq, the marsh Arabs are opposed to the the Iraqi government and have sided with the country's enemies during wars. In the 1980s, Saddam Hussein began to divert water away from the area, and most of the land has now dried up or turned to mud. In a few years, the marsh Arabs have gone from a thriving culture to almost total ruin.

In Southeast Asia, rice paddies form artificial wetlands. In hilly places, such as Bali (below), people build flat steps called terraces on the hills to trap rain in the paddies.

Farmers set young rice plants by hand, carefully spacing them apart in rows. In Bali, the farmers wear umbrella-shaped hats to keep off the rain.

sometimes used stilts to wade through the water, and in winter they got around with the help of another useful invention—ice skates.

Floodplains and Farming

Wetlands were crucial to the development of farming. People seem to have begun growing crops around 10,000 years ago. A few thousand years later, farmers began growing crops in river floodplains, such as that of the Nile in Egypt. The Nile used to flood every year, so the ancient Egyptians devised an elaborate system of mud banks to trap the floodwater in flat fields. This soaked the ground and allowed the muddy river sediment to settle, making the soil very fertile. Farming on floodplains also developed in ancient China and other places, though these farmers relied on year-round irrigation systems rather than the river's natural floods.

 # Stolen Plumes

In the late 1800s, women's fashion nearly wiped out some of the world's showiest wetland birds, all for the sake of their feathers. One of these birds was a beautiful, pure-white type of heron called the snowy egret (below). The law eventually protected it in its Everglades home in 1897, but even after that date, at least two game wardens were killed by feather-poachers. As a result of protection, the egret's numbers recovered, only to be hit hard by pollution later in the 20th century.

The Shrinking Everglades

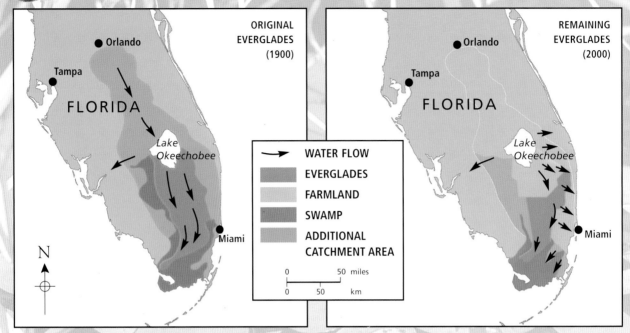

ORIGINAL EVERGLADES (1900)

Orlando

Tampa

FLORIDA

Lake Okeechobee

Miami

N

REMAINING EVERGLADES (2000)

Orlando

Tampa

FLORIDA

Lake Okeechobee

Miami

WATER FLOW
EVERGLADES
FARMLAND
SWAMP
ADDITIONAL CATCHMENT AREA

0   50 miles
0   50 km

The Everglades once formed an immensely wide river of saw grass that flowed very slowly from Lake Okeechobee to the sea. The area of land that contributed water to the Everglades—its catchment area—was very large, and it is shown in olive in the left map. Since then, people have diverted much of the water toward newly drained farmland (in yellow on the right map) and toward the growing cities. A lot less water now reaches the Everglades, and the water supply is irregular and often polluted. Measures are now underway to manage the water better. By reducing waste and storing water in reservoirs, people can keep the remaining Everglades steadily supplied with clean water, as it was before 1900.

Large-scale farming systems need somebody to organize them, and to make sure nobody takes more than his or her fair share of water. Some historians believe that this kind of farming is the reason major civilizations developed in the first place—complete with bureaucrats, cities, and tax collectors.

Farming can change a wetland enormously, and sometimes it stops being a wetland at all. This is less true, though, for the world's most important cereal crop: rice. Rice is a true wetland plant. Farmers often plant it in flooded fields called paddies, which are surrounded by low banks to keep the water trapped. In other places, rice is grown on natural floodplains—some varieties of rice can grow up to 8 inches (20 cm) a day to keep pace with rising floodwater.

Paddies form a kind of artificial wetland covering much of the land in eastern and southern Asia. Some of this is at the expense of natural wetlands, but people have also built rice paddies on the sides of mountains, creating wetlands where tropical rain forests once grew. Although less rich in wildlife than natural wetlands or rain forests, rice paddies can still be important habitats. Farmers often stock them with fish, and they also provide homes for frogs, snakes, migrating waterbirds, and other animals.

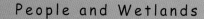
Cranberries are grown in artificial marshes with acidic, peaty soil. At harvest time, the marshes are flooded to help collect the fruit, which is then loaded into trucks.

Drainage and Destruction

In the past, people saw wetlands as unhealthy places—sometimes with good reason, because many are infested with mosquitoes and leeches. But it was not until recent centuries that people began to destroy wetlands on a large scale. For example, half of the wetlands in the United States (excluding Alaska) disappeared since Europeans arrived and began converting wetlands to farmland.

Huge areas of mangrove swamps have been cut down throughout the tropics—sometimes for their wood, sometimes so that the land can be used for shrimp farms. In cooler countries, people have damaged or destroyed bogs by digging up the peat they contain. Although peat has always been used on a small scale for fuel in countries such as Ireland, peat-extraction has become a major industry in some places. In Finland, there is even a peat-fired power station.

People have also damaged wetlands by allowing polluted water to enter them. In the Florida Everglades, pollution from farm fertilizers has been a particular problem. The saw grass plant that dominates the Everglades thrives in water low in nutrients. Fertilizers add nutrients to the water, allowing other plants, such as cattails, to take over.

When we damage wetlands, it's not only the plants and animals living there that suffer. We also deny ourselves the benefits that wetlands naturally provide. One benefit is flood protection—without wetlands, we run the risk of catastrophic floods.

Good and Bad Floods

It's natural for rivers to flood; some do it every year, others less often. Rivers that flood regularly often have wetlands around them, but when we try to control the flooding, we destroy the wetlands. In the western United States, for example, dams built to control floods have led to the disapparance of cottonwood forests beside many rivers.

Wetlands themselves can help control floods. By absorbing water, they stop a large flood from turning into a catastrophe. Upstream wetlands can soak up heavy rain so it does not get into the river so quickly. Downstream on the floodplain, wetlands provide room for floodwater to spill out, rather than channeling it between narrow banks. The disastrous 1993 Mississippi flood,

The Peace-Athabasca Delta

On the shores of Lake Athabasca in Alberta, Canada, is a huge wetland area: the Peace–Athabasca Delta. It's one of North America's most important sites for migrating waterbirds. The delta relies on natural floods that take place every year, but in 1968 a dam on the Peace River nearly shut off the floods. Almost immediately, trees began to take over from marshland plants, destroying the habitat the waterbirds needed. Fortunately, the authorities responded and altered the way the new system worked, partly re-creating the original floods.

The Mississippi Delta is a vast area of wetlands, enriched by river sediment. So much sediment washes out to sea that it can even be seen from space (inset).

which killed 50 people and left 70,000 homeless, was all the worse because vast areas of the Mississippi's original wetlands had been destroyed. A system of dams and levees (banks) had been built to keep water in the river, but these defenses were overwhelmed by heavy rains in the summer of 1993. Afterward, many people said that the dams and levees had made the floods worse because they channeled all the floodwater into the disaster zone. Since 1993, there has been a move to re-create some of the Mississippi's original wetlands.

Likewise, coastal wetlands can protect against flooding from the sea, and can reduce the erosion (wearing away of the land) that floods cause. The tangled roots of mangrove trees are especially good at absorbing the energy of storm waves, which would otherwise wash ashore and do great damage.

Pure Water

When water flows through a wetland, it often comes out purer than when it went in. As long as the water is not so polluted that it damages the wetland, we can all benefit from this natural form of water treatment. Fertilizers in water, for example, are removed by wetland plants or by bacteria living among the plants' roots. Some wetlands, such as

In wet or marshy places, like Bangkok in Thailand, stilts give houses extra stability as well as keeping them dry.

bogs, are very good at holding onto chemicals called heavy metals, preventing them from getting into drinking water.

People have set up various systems to make use of the purifying properties of wetlands. One, adopted by the water authorities in New York City, is simply to buy and preserve the wetlands that lie around the sources of the city's water supply. In many parts of the world, people use beds of reeds to purify their sewage water. Another well-established system is the use of wetlands containing water hyacinth plants to purify water polluted by heavy metals. The plants absorb these toxic chemicals and are then scooped up and thrown away.

Added Value

There are many other benefits to be had from wetlands. For example, by trapping heavy rain, wetlands give water time to percolate into the ground and fill up underground water stores. Peat bogs remove carbon

dioxide gas from the air as the plants grow, helping reduce global warming (see page 59). When the plants die, the carbon dioxide stays trapped in their dead remains (peat). Some wetlands, especially on the coast, provide vital food and shelter for young fish—without such wetlands, stocks of fish in the sea would plummet. And even today, harvesting from wetlands—collecting reeds for roofs, for example—remains important.

Many people enjoy the natural beauty of wetland landscapes and wildlife. In places such as the Florida Everglades and the Okavango Delta in Africa, visiting ecotourists have become important to the local economy. For scientists, wetlands (especially bogs) are also historical records— by digging down into them, you can find evidence of what Earth's plants and climate were like thousands of years ago. It's not easy to put a dollar value on all these benefits, but the world would be a poorer place for sure if the wetlands disappeared.

Far from being disease-ridden swamps, many wetland areas are now major tourist attractions. In the wet season, air boats give visitors a thrilling tour across the saw grass rivers in the Everglades.

Sundarbans

The world's largest river delta is where the Brahmaputra and Ganges rivers of Asia flow into the Bay of Bengal. Where the delta meets the sea is a vast mangrove forest called the Sundarbans, interwoven with miles of saltwater creeks.

 ## Fact File

▲ In the late 1970s, tigers killed around 45 people every year in the Sundarbans.

▲ People have cut down most of Asia's forests, so the Sundarbans is an important haven for wildlife.

▲ Animals include three rare members of the cat family: tigers, fishing cats, and jungle cats. Other animals include mongooses and monkeys.

 ## The Royal Bengal Tiger

The Sundarbans is home to the largest population of tigers now left in the wild. Although tigers are all one species, the local variety is given its own name—the royal Bengal tiger. Their main food is wild boar, but they also eat people. Visitors to the forest often pray to a local god or goddess to protect them from the tigers. They sometimes wear face masks on the back of their heads to scare off tigers, and they leave electrified human dummies in the forest to repulse tigers from attacking people.

Because mangrove trees grow in waterlogged mud, their roots get little air. To make up for the shortfall, vertical roots that work like snorkels grow upward from the ground. The roots have small holes called lenticels, which let air enter. Hollows inside the root allow the air to circulate deep underground.

1. Farmland
Mangrove swamps and forests once covered nearly the whole area of this map, but most have been cut down and replaced by farmland (pale colors), such as rice paddies.

2. Mangroves
Dense mangrove forests appear bright green.

3. Sundarbans Wildlife Sanctuaries (Bangladesh)
Three small areas of the Bangladeshi Sundarbans are preserved as wildlife sanctuaries. Outside these areas, logging and other commercial activities take place.

4. Sundarbans
The Sundarbans has a total area of about 4,000 square miles (10,000 sq km), half of which is tidal creeks and waterways.

5. Silt
Vast amounts of silt (muddy particles) are carried into the Bay of Bengal by the many rivers flowing through the delta. The silt provides nutrients for mangrove trees.

6. Sundarbans Tiger Reserve (India)
Between Matla River and the border with Bangladesh is a reserve for the royal Bengal tiger. Part of the reserve is a national park, where commercial activities are illegal.

7. Calcutta
The southern neighborhoods of Calcutta appear as a dark area. Calcutta is India's largest city, with a population of 13 million. It is the nearest major city to the Sundarbans.

8. Bay of Bengal
Part of the Indian Ocean, the Bay of Bengal is the source of tropical storms that regularly batter the delta region.

9. Hugli River
The center of Calcutta (not in map area) is on the east bank of this river, about 96 miles (154 km) upstream from the Bay of Bengal.

N

CHINA

INDIA

SOUTHEAST ASIA

Farmland

1

Farmland

2

Mangroves

Haringhat River

● Mungla

B A N G L A D E S H

Kanga River

3

Sundarbans wildlife sanctuaries

S u n d a r b a n s

4

I N D I A

5

Silt

National border

7

Calcutta

6

Sundarbans Tiger Reserve

Matla River

8

Bay of Bengal

Hugli River

9

0   20 miles
0   20 km

The Future

Wetlands will continue to face threats in the future, but many countries are now taking action to protect and restore them.

The good news for wetlands is that we now understand a lot better how they work—and what can happen when we interfere with them. Gone are the days when a developed country could put up a massive dam without stopping to think how it might affect the natural environment downstream. On the other hand, on our increasingly crowded planet, many wetlands are going to remain under pressure from human development for the foreseeable future.

Wetlands Under Threat

Some of the threats to wetlands are familiar ones that apply to most biomes. For example, illegal hunting of animals such as crocodiles

The city of Gold Coast in Australia is a futuristic mixture of wetland and town. More than 250 miles (400 km) of rivers and waterways weave among its skyscrapers and residential streets.

and jaguars for their skins is still common in many places. People also continue to drain wetlands so that they can be turned into farmland. From time to time, wetland plants and animals escape from places such as ornamental gardens and fur farms, only to become pests in wetlands where they never lived before. An example is purple loosestrife, a garden plant native to European wetlands. In the 19th century it escaped from gardens in North America and began to infest waterways and wetlands, where it now crowds out the natural plant life.

Water Power

Other threats come from our ever-increasing need for electricity and water. Dams are not just built to stop rivers from flooding—they also provide electricity. In a hydroelectric power station, some of the water trapped behind the dam is allowed down huge pipes, driving rotating machines called turbines as it flows. The turbines convert the energy of the moving water into electricity.

Hydroelectric dams deprive wetlands downstream of water, but people need to build them. Poor countries, especially, are desperate for the cheap, renewable electricity that hydropower produces. People will also continue to divert rivers to irrigate fields, even though irrigation can make the soil too salty for plants to grow. In some parts of the world, water is such a precious resource that countries might even end up going to war to control rivers.

Another threat to the world's wetlands is global warming. This process is caused by certain gases, called greenhouse gases, that build up in the atmosphere and trap the sun's heat. Carbon dioxide gas from burning coal

The Ramsar Convention

In 1971, scientists and officials from all over the world held a conference in the town of Ramsar in Iran to discuss the future of wetlands. The result of this conference was an agreement between a number of countries to try and protect their wetlands and to encourage others to do so. Each new country that signs up to the convention has to nominate at least one wetland area that it will protect. For example, the United States started by nominating the Florida Everglades. There are now more than 1,000 Ramsar sites all over the world.

Saving the Everglades

One of the biggest wetland restoration projects in the world is currently underway in Florida. For many years, polluted water has been seeping into the Everglades from farmland to the north. The water contains chemical fertilizers, which change the kinds of plants growing in the Everglades and thus deprive animals of their natural food. The National Park authorities tried to make local farmers stop using fertilizers, but the farmers wouldn't agree. After years of lawsuits, the park and the farmers finally settled their differences and signed the Everglades Forever Act of 1994. Under the terms of the act, the State of Florida has to construct a vast area of filtration marshes between the farmland and the Everglades. These marshes will clean the water by absorbing any fertilizers. As a result, farmers can carry on using chemicals, and the water flowing into the Everglades will be pure.

and oil is the main culprit. Its effects may already be with us—ice is melting near the poles, and sea levels are beginning to rise. Over the coming century, many coastal wetlands could end up under the sea.

One danger of global warming is that it might lead to an environmental vicious circle that could destroy the peat bogs of Russia, Canada, and Alaska. The warmer the weather, the more the peat dries out—and the more likely it is to catch fire. If peat burns, it releases more carbon dioxide into the atmosphere, fueling global warming.

Some wetlands, especially rice paddies, might be making global warming worse. The culprit in this case is methane gas, which is released when dead plants rot. Like carbon dioxide, methane is a greenhouse gas.

The London Wetland Centre (below) is a massive artificial wetland built on the site of four disused reservoirs (left) in London, England. Biologists calculate the site is home to 140 bird species, 18 dragonfly and damselfly species, at least 260 moth species, 4 amphibian species, 4 bat species, and one water vole species—and all in one of the world's biggest cities.

Hopes for the Future

Many countries are now trying to improve and manage their wetlands. In the United States, this involves a policy of "no net loss"—if people destroy or build on a wetland, they have to create a new one elsewhere. People are not yet sure how to create wetlands, though. Some think the best technique is to flood the land and leave the rest to nature, while others believe that deliberate planting helps the process along.

Dams are now being demolished and built at the same rate in the United States, and natural flooding is being allowed to take place again on certain rivers. This follows a 1996 experiment on the Colorado River, when floodwater deliberately released from a dam helped re-create riverside wetlands.

Large wetlands may also eventually be restored around the Mississippi River to help control flooding. There is even a proposal to join these wetlands to make a Mississippi Wetlands National Park, stretching through much of the Midwest. With ecotourism growing throughout the world, such a move might help the region's economy, too.

Below: This artificial wetland in Wicomico County, Maryland, provides a stopover for migrating waterbirds.

Glossary

amphibian: An animal that lives partly in water and partly on land, such as a frog, toad, or salamander.

atmosphere: The layer of air around Earth.

bald cypress: A tree with a wide, spreading base that is common in North American swamps.

biome: A major division of the living world, distinguished by its climate and wildlife. Tundra, desert, and temperate grasslands are examples of biomes.

bog: A type of wetland in which partly decayed plant matter builds up in soggy, acidic ground. Bogs usually form in cold, rainy places.

carbon dioxide: A gas released when fuel burns. Carbon dioxide is one of the main gases thought to cause global warming.

cattail: Any member of a reedlike family of plants whose flowers look like cigars on sticks.

climate: The pattern of weather that happens in one place during an average year.

conifer: A type of plant that does not have true fruit like flowering plants but instead produces seeds protected inside a cone. Conifers often have needle-shaped leaves.

delta: A wide, typically Δ-shaped plain at the mouth of a river where sediment collects.

ecosystem: A collection of living animals and plants that function together with their environment. Ecosystems include food chains.

emergent: A wetland plant that has roots and a stem underwater but leaves in the air.

equator: An imaginary line around Earth, midway between the North and South poles.

erosion: The gradual wearing away of land by the action of wind, rain, rivers, ice, or the sea.

evaporate: To turn into gas. When water evaporates, it becomes an invisible part of the air.

fen: A type of wetland that forms where water from the ground spreads over low, flat land. Fens occur in temperate countries.

fertile: Capable of sustaining plant growth. Farmers often try to make soil more fertile when growing crops.

fertilizer: A chemical used by farmers to make land more fertile.

gills: Organs that enable aquatic animals to breathe underwater.

global warming: The gradual warming of Earth's climate, thought to be caused by pollution of the atmosphere.

ice age: A period when Earth's climate was cooler and the polar ice caps expanded. The last ice age ended 10,000 years ago.

infertile: Soil that is unable to support plentiful plant life is termed infertile.

irrigation: The use of channeled water by people to grow plants in dry areas.

lagoon: An area of calm, shallow water partly separated from the sea or a lake by a stretch of land.

mangrove: A tree that grows in swamps on tropical coasts. Many mangroves have prop roots to support themselves.

marsh: A type of wetland that mostly contains small, grassy plants, such as reeds.

migration: A long-distance journey by an animal to find a new home. Many animals migrate each year.

nutrient: Any chemical that nourishes plants or animals, helping them grow. Plants absorb nutrients from the soil, while animals get nutrients from food.

oxbow lake: A curved lake that was once a bend in a river.

oxygen: A gas in the air. Animals and plants need to take in oxygen so that their cells can release energy from food.

peat: Partly decayed dead plant matter that builds up in bogs.

pollen: A dustlike powder produced by the male parts of flowers.

pollination: The transfer of pollen from the male part of a flower to the female part of the same flower or another flower, causing the flower to produce seeds.

prairie: A large area of grassland in central North America.

predator: An animal that catches and eats other animals.

protein: One of the major food groups. It is used for building and repairing plant and animal bodies.

rain forest: A lush forest that receives frequent heavy rainfall. Tropical rain forests grow in the tropics; temperate rain forests grow in cooler places.

reed: A tall member of the grass family, common in wetlands and riverbanks. Sedges and cattails are sometimes incorrectly called reeds.

salt marsh: A type of wetland that forms on low-lying coasts in temperate countries.

saw grass: A type of sedge common in the Florida Everglades. Its leaves have rows of sharp teeth set into the edges.

sedge: Any member of a family of grasslike plants that typically have stiff, almost solid stems.

species: A particular type of organism. Cheetahs are a species, for instance, but birds are not, because there are lots of different bird species.

swamp: A shallow wetland full of trees that can grow in water.

temperate: Having a moderate climate. Earth's temperate zone lies between the warm tropical regions and the cold, polar regions.

tropic of Cancer: An imaginary line around Earth 1,600 miles (2,600 km) north of the equator. From here, the Sun is directly overhead at noon on June 21.

tropic of Capricorn: An imaginary line around Earth about 1,600 miles (2,600 km) south of the equator.

tropical: Between the tropics of Cancer and Capricorn. Tropical countries are warm all year.

tropical forest: Forest in Earth's tropical zone, such as tropical rain forest or monsoon forest.

tropical grassland: A tropical biome in which grass is the main form of plant life.

tundra: A biome of the far north, made up of treeless plains covered with small plants.

Further Research

Books

Doyle, Arthur Conan. *The Hound of the Baskervilles*. New York: Signet Classics, 2001.
(The famous detective novel featuring Sherlock Holmes, in which a sinister English wetland in Devon, the Grimpen Mire, plays an important role.)
Finlayson, Max, and Moser, Michael (editors). *Wetlands*. New York: Facts on File, 1991.
Goulding, Michael. *Amazon: The Flooded Forest*. London: BBC Books, 1989.
Hancock, James. *Birds of the Wetlands*. San Diego, CA: Academic Press, 1999.
Thesiger, Wilfred. *The Marsh Arabs*. New York: Dutton, 1964.

Websites

U.S. Environmental Protection Agency: www.epa.gov/OWOW/wetlands/vital/toc.html
(An easy-to-use site giving information about wetlands in the United States and worldwide.)
The Everglades Ecosystem: www.nps.gov/ever/eco/
(Information about the Everglades from the U.S. National Park Service.)
Chesapeake Bay Program: www.chesapeakebay.net/
(Find out more about one of the premier coastal wetland sites in the United States.)

Index

Picture Credits